The World of Wolves

A Piccolo Book Pan Books Ltd London and Sydney

Jacquelyn Berrill
The World of Wolves

Illustrated by the author

First published in Great Britain 1972 as
Wonders of the World of Wolves by World's Work Ltd
This edition published 1975 by Pan Books Ltd,
Cavaye Place, London SW10 9PG
ISBN 0 330 24291 1
© Jacquelyn Berrill 1970

Printed in Great Britain by
Richard Clay (The Chaucer Press) Ltd, Bungay, Suffolk

Contents

Wolf portrait

Introduction

It is believed that all dogs have descended from wolves whose pictures, alongside the hunters, were painted 50,000 years ago on the walls of caves. By the time the Egyptians built their monuments, 4,000 to 5,000 years ago, several breeds of dogs had been developed. Tall, slender dogs and short-legged ones were cut into their stone decorations. Your pet dog and the wolf may look different, but they are the same in the details upon which scientists base relationships — details such as having identical teeth.

The only member of the wolf family now living wild in Britain is the red fox. I want to tell you about the timber wolf, the coyote, and the red fox, three members of this family which still live wild in North America.

It is because the most beautiful of the dog family, the wolf, is becoming extinct that I have decided to tell its story. Scientists who actually study the wolf in its environment have quite a different tale to relate from the one you may find in your storybooks. It is their discovery that the wolf is a shy and intelligent creature and far from being the villain that we have been led to believe.

I have chosen to describe the timber wolf because the scientific studies of this wild dog are numerous, but all wolves are essentially the same. The timber wolf is usually gray, but ranges in color from black to silver. He lives in Alaska, Northern Canada and in the Rockies. In different parts of the world he is called by other names. Generally speaking, in the North the fur is longer and thicker and the animal larger and more powerful

7

than in the South, where the wolf is also darker in color. We find the black wolf in Florida and the red wolf in Texas and the dusty wolf in the central plains. The arctic wolf is white with a black tail tip. Since the creatures wearing the different colored coats are the same, I need only tell you about the habits of one, the timber wolf.

I have, however, decided to include the story of the coyote, who is really a small wolf about the size of a setter dog. Sometimes this small dog relative is called a prairie wolf or even a red wolf, depending on where you live. Because the coyote is so widespread, you may know this small wolf and have been thrilled by its call. Unless legislation is passed to protect all the wild creatures, this small wolf may be the only wolf left. If he survives it will be because he is so intelligent.

The fox is another dog relative whose future is in jeopardy, although in the past foxes have been able to spread all over the world. I have included the story of the red fox, but he may be seen wearing a coat of pure black or silver. All foxes are similar, but gray foxes are more timid than red and prefer dense thickets. Kit foxes live in deserts, and the arctic fox, gray in summer and white in winter, has smaller ears and a blunt face. The so-called "blue fox" is but a color phase of the arctic fox. Foxes may prefer to live near farmlands, wood lots, dense forests, marshlands, even cities, but there is little variation in their behavior, so in this book the red fox is used as an example.

These creatures are all related to your dog, but they have an added interest because they are a part of our wild heritage and as such are especially precious today. Have you ever thought of what our world would be like without our wild animals? The fate of these creatures and others as well is in your hands, the future citizens of the world. It is up to YOU to stop their destruction before it is too late.

To all children who care for
the wildlife around them

The Timber Wolf

Less than a hundred years ago the timber wolf could be found throughout North America wherever there was wilderness to give it protection. Today there are no wolves left in forty-five states, and outside of Alaska there are probably less than 500 individual wolves living in Minnesota, Wisconsin, and Michigan together. Just as a drained pond cannot support fish, a destroyed wilderness cannot support wolves.

America's first settlers found wilderness aplenty where all manner of wild creatures lived, and the hunter and the hunted raised their young in balance with nature. The very word *wilderness* means "wild-deer-home." Where there were wild deer the wolves also lived, finding plenty of food by attacking only the weakest of the herds. The great antlered deer, strong and fleet, lived to raise healthy young.

The settlers brought their livestock, and wolves, finding cattle fenced in, discovered food handy and naturally attacked the creatures so easily obtained. The wolf's digestive system requires fresh meat—and only meat. The deer, on the other hand, can eat only plants, and man has a stomach that can manage meat and plants alike. The difference is that when man wants meat he leaves the job of butchering to someone else, while he looks the other way. Wolves have to do the job themselves.

When livestock was killed, the farmer said that the wolf must be eliminated—and he was. Man cleared the wilderness and spread out across the land, trapping, hunting, and poisoning the wolves as he went. Even the remote wilderness of the Far West offered no safety, for man feared that the wolves would come down into the cattle and sheep country and so they were pursued and killed even in their last hiding place.

Today only a few of the beautiful wild creatures live in the Sierra Nevada and when stragglers come down from Canada they are quickly killed. Throughout the United States the few wolves that remain and feed on wild prey, as is their nature, have bounties on their heads because the so-called sportsman with his gun feels that the animals killed by the wolves for food are game animals and as such should be man's sport to kill.

The large size of the wolf makes it a good target, and its habit of howling and of hunting in packs makes the creature seem evil to those who are ignorant. But is the wolf evil? There is no proof that any wolf, with the exception of an animal suffering from rabies, has ever attacked a human being in North America. Dogs sometimes get rabies, but we do not condemn all dogs as evil. So why do we hate and fear the wolf?

As youngsters we learned to think of the wolf as a most undesirable creature. Remember the story of "The Three Little Pigs"? Who was it that huffed and puffed and blew the house in? We sang "Who's Afraid of the Big Bad Wolf?" as we marched about pretending to be brave. We grew up hearing about "Little Red Riding Hood" and the wolf with a large mouth, "the better to eat you with." And by the time we started to school we were familiar with the story and music of *Peter and the Wolf* and pretended that we had single-handedly tied up the bad wolf.

These are all very old stories that came to us from northern Europe and may have been a result of a situation that really existed in the Middle Ages. Between the twelfth and fourteenth centuries the weather became very cold in northern Europe, so

The arctic wolf in his white coat that matches the snow differs little from the timber wolf

cold that the game animals that furnished much of the food could not exist, and starvation resulted among people and all the creatures who depend on meat—including wolves.

Wolves hunt in packs and a starving pack of wolves must have been terrifying. The fight to survive is great in all animals, and just as a starving man would eat anything, so would a starving pack of wolves attack a man.

Out of those lean years grew a fear of the wolf and out of that fear came the stories of wolves attacking people. But that was in Europe six hundred years ago. Still, those stories became the nursery tales handed down to us. Few heard about the strong, intelligent wolf or the brave and beautiful wolf. It was only the bad wolf!

There are some other much older stories about wolves that saved the lives of young children, nursed and protected them, even raised them. One such story goes way back to Rome and its myths.

Romulus and Remus, twin sons of the god Mars, were placed by a wicked uncle in a trough and set adrift on the Tiber River. The trough grounded in the marshes where the little boy babies were suckled by a she-wolf. When they grew up they learned their true identity and founded the city of Rome where they had been raised by the kind wolf. The wolf was the sacred beast of the god Mars and his den was a holy spot. So, long ago, the wolf was not an enemy, but a creature regarded as being strong, kind, and intelligent, as indeed the wolf really is.

What is the truth about the wolf? First, the wolf is a killer. It is his nature to kill, for he must have fresh meat to live and he, unlike man, has no one to kill for him. Then, the wolf howls and this weird sound frightens many people, but the wolf is only communicating with his own kind, calling to keep in touch or just singing for the joy of it. It is a thrilling wild call. And the wolf is a chaser of moving objects. The hunting wolf must run alongside the fleeing animal until it is outdistanced or the creature weakens. Yes, the wolf chases, but so do dogs, and the wolf is a dog too, a very close relative of your pet. A dog chasing a car is not angry but thrilled with the chase. Any story about a wolf chasing a man probably rises from the fact that the man ran first. The wolf, like the dog, pursues him.

If you add to all this the fact that the wolf did not know the difference between wild and domestic meat, you can see why the early settlers in America, who did not understand, took such a dislike to the wolf. The government, at their insistence, put a

The wolf is strong, intelligent, and beautiful

bounty on wolves; that is, paid money for each dead wolf. Every wolf in the wild is now killed for money or for so-called sport, and as a result one of the most intelligent creatures that ever existed may pass from this earth in your lifetime unless we begin to protect it.

What is happening in the states that still have a few wolves living in their woodlands? Michigan removed its bounty in 1958 but has an open season, which means that during that time wolves can be killed on sight at any time for sport, not money. Wisconsin removed its bounty and only part of the year can wolves be hunted. Minnesota, the state that boasts of its great wilderness and has about 300 to 400 wolves left, still has a bounty.

In Canada and Alaska, the Indians and Eskimos, the wolf, the caribou, and the moose lived together for hundreds of years in perfect balance, with each adding its richness to the wilderness landscape. But times have changed. While the wolf is protected in Mt. McKinley National Park and has been since 1950, outside the park borders a poisoning program and hunting from airplanes take a heavy toll of the wolves.

Once the wolf faced only the man with a gun; then came the aircraft and now the great "sportsman" can follow a pack and shoot every individual in it from the air. Yet even worse things are happening. The snowmobile has come into the hands of these "sportsmen" and wolf tracks can be followed to the nursery den. The wolf has no chance at all unless he is given protection. Otherwise, the voice of the wolf will be silenced across the land.

Would you like to meet a timber wolf family and see how it lives in its wilderness home?

The heavy, dark gray wolf trots along the well-packed path in the snow at the edge of the ice-covered lake. In the late afternoon sun the wolf's coat looks almost blue and his heavy mane shines like silver around his black face. He pauses long enough to let his mate catch up with him and then, leading the way, he climbs the gravel ridge. In spite of his short legs and weight, there is a spring in his step and his tail wags happily.

Wolves walk along the edge of an ice-covered lake

His mate follows more slowly. Her coat is a lighter gray and the markings on her face make her appear to be wearing a black mask. She is more slender than her mate and she moves gracefully along the trail toward the top of the ridge.

Halfway up, the large gray wolf pauses again, this time by a newly dug hole. The slender female approaches him with her head low and with sideways dancing steps until she touches his

The wolf disappears into a prospective den

shoulder. Then she disappears into the hole and soon reappears
with her tail wagging and follows her mate along the trail.

A mile farther along, both wolves enter a dug-out hole in the
ridge but soon appear again and continue their upward journey.
These are extra dens the wolves have cleaned out to be used in
an emergency while raising their pups. They are homes to come
to in case of danger, or to move to when a clean house is needed,
or when a nursery den becomes too crowded.

When the pair reaches the foot of a steep bluff near the top of
the gravel ridge the large wolf points his black face upward and
gives a long drawn-out call. The notes start low and move slowly
up the scale with increased volume. There is a slight break at the
highest point, followed by a deep throaty tone and a gradual
descent of the scale until it ends on a long soft note. Almost at
once two half-grown wolves dash down the ridge, slipping and
sliding, their tails wagging madly. These are the young of the
year before. The first to reach the parents is a light gray male,

She follows her mate up the ridge

The female approaches her mate with dancing steps

buff underneath, with long rust-colored hairs in his thick gray mane.

The slender, nearly black female arrives almost as soon. She hugs the older male with her long forelegs and pushes her thin muzzle into his heavy ruff. The young male rolls on his back while both give throaty barks. The large wolf holds his tail high and licks their faces. The older female joins in the face-licking and paw-hugging, for this is a joyful reunion of the family and one that takes place after any separation, be it long or short.

All four sit with shoulders touching and noses pointed skyward and give long musical howls of pleasure. They "sing" for several minutes and no doubt can be heard for many miles. When the last low note dies, the large wolf leads the way up the steep bluff to the entrance of their den.

The young wolves curl up on the flat ledge near the opening; the strong male continues to a spot above the den and stretches out on the snow to keep watch; the female drops to her belly and crawls into the opening and along the tunnel for several feet until it becomes large enough for her to stand erect. The passage widens in several places, obviously sleeping places for the wolf family. The long tunnel turns and divides many times, but she walks along to a circular room soon to be the nursery where she will raise her new family. She turns around a few times, as you have seen her dog relatives do, and then curls up to sleep.

This den was first dug and used by a fox family. Other occupants enlarged it. This is the second year this pair of wolves have used it. They, too, have changed the den to make it more comfortable.

At sunset the female is aroused by a howl at the entrance and she quickly joins her mate. She licks his face and he licks hers.

The wolf yearlings

She rolls over in front of him and fondles his mane with her paws. They are joined by their two almost-grown pups with their tails wagging and their heads held low. Their throaty barks cease and they join their parents in chorus. The voices float out on the clear evening air as they "sing" for the pure joy of it.

Abruptly the large male starts down the steep incline, followed closely by his mate and the energetic young of the year before. These two, although as large as their parents, are slight, gangling, awkward, immature wolves with still much to be learned from their parents before they leave the family group.

At the bottom of the slope the male wolf turns and howls. The others come close, with tails wagging and much nose-touching, and join them in another short singsong.

The female watches as her mate and the young wolves depart for a night of hunting. She is as good a hunter as her mate, but today she sees them disappear into the twilight. She points her muzzle up and gives a long drawn-out call and hears their reply from far away before she turns and walks slowly up the ridge to the den. She knows it is too near the time for her pups to be born for her to risk leaving. Although it is May, snow still covers the land; only the wind-swept ridges are clear. In the dim twilight the woods below are black. She gives one last high-pitched call before she drops to her knees and crawls into the den.

It is not yet daylight when she is awakened by a distant howl, and she rushes to the entrance to return the call. She receives several responses, each one nearer and nearer. She looks in the direction of the calls, her ears high, her body trembling with excitement, and her tail wagging. Finally, when she can stand it no longer, she barks and rushes down the steep slope to meet the returning hunters.

With head lowered she approaches her mate and rolls on her side before him with both paws on his shoulder. He drops the

The wolves point their noses skyward and give a long musical howl

fresh meat he carries in his strong jaws and touches noses with her. His tail is held high. The two yearlings rush forward, drop the meat they carry, and dance about touching noses with the others. Now, all together, they tell the world that they have returned safely after a successful hunt and bring food for the one who waited. It is a glorious sound to usher in a new day. The hunters pick up their burdens and, single file, the four wolves climb the ridge to the den.

At the entrance they place their contributions before the hungry wolf, who begins to eat ravenously. The young animals walk about fifty feet away and curl up. Their stomachs are full and they are soon asleep. The older male climbs to the very top of the ridge and stretches out with his head on his paws. He has a good view of the countryside for miles around in all directions. His

She barks and rushes down the slope

eyes close and he sleeps for a few minutes, then raises his head
and looks about, and sleeps again. From this place he guards his
family.

He is a good provider for the mate he has taken for life—and a
good parent as well. Until his mate can travel again with him, he
must hunt for both of them. When the pups arrive he dares not
leave long enough to reach the herds of deer, but must be con-
tent with smaller creatures nearby and the caches of food he has
placed close enough to reach in a short time. His long hunting
trips are over for a while.

Down in the nursery, six sooty brown pups are born on the bare earth. They are like balls of thick fur and look like small dogs—but why not, when they are so closely related? Their eyes are tightly closed but they know how to suck and when the mother wolf has licked them clean they have their first meal of warm milk, and then go to sleep.

The wolf mother could have had more or fewer pups. The size of her litter depends on the abundance of food available. When food is scarce, litters are small. It is nature's way of controlling the number of pups born when times are hard.

For the first few weeks the mother stays almost constantly with her helpless babies, feeding and keeping them warm and safe. She leaves them briefly to eat the food her mate and the yearlings bring to the entrance of the den. Between the fifth and ninth day the pups open their blue eyes. They can't see much in the dark den, but they crawl about over their mother and each other. They nurse often and fall asleep again when they are filled.

The hungry mother wolf, stiff from lying on her side so long, crawls on her belly out of the nursery room and along the tunnel. At the entrance she finds snow blocking the doorway. She scratches with her paws until she pushes aside the snowdrift and stands looking out on a white world. This is a severe storm for May—all familiar landmarks are gone. Usually there are fresh tracks leading away from the den in the evening and toward the den in the morning, made by the returning hunters. There are no tracks this morning.

She searches in every direction for the sight of moving figures in the early morning light. The female is very thin from the almost constant nursing of the six pups. Her gray hair hangs loose on her sides. She is very hungry, and worried too. She points her black masked muzzle upward and gives a long mournful sound. She listens, but there is no answering call. Back and forth she

Snow blocks the entrance of the den

walks, making whimpering noises in her throat. She licks melting snow from her shoulder hairs, for she is thirsty too. Her babies get all the liquid they need from her milk, but she must drink. She eats some snow and again scans the landscape in the direction in which the hunters had departed. Hunger had forced her mate to go far in search of fresh meat.

Her body becomes tense. Is that a movement she sees on the top of a distant ridge? Is it a bear, a fox—or her hunters? She gives a loud howl. There is an answer, and then another. Now she can recognize the yearling wolves. She moves about nervously, looking in every direction. She does not see her mate. She barks loudly and rushes down the slope, sending loose snow flying in every direction.

When she meets the young wolves she pauses to lick their faces. All tails wag and there is a very brief chorus of greeting

calls that ends abruptly. Her mate is missing. She looks toward
the den where her babies sleep and even takes a few steps in that
direction before she whirls about and gives a sharp bark and
leaps forward down the ridge along the tracks made by the
young wolves. She slips and slides downward on her stomach toward the dense black woods. She stops and listens. A clear call
tells her the young wolves are on guard at the den. Then there is
a faint short call not far away. She answers in a high voice and
turns toward the woods.

She is up to her thighs in loose drifts and progress is slow and
hard. She pauses to get her breath and to call once more. This
time she hears again the answer she wants and follows the tracks
toward the frozen lake.

Suddenly she sees her strong mate lying still against the white
snow. He tries to stand. She noses him down and licks his face
and then his injured leg. Large blocks of ice piled on the shore
and deep blue patches of water tell her the story. Her heavy
mate had crashed through the thin ice.

After a while she nuzzles him to his feet and, making whim-

The wolf finds the going hard

27

pering sounds and wagging her tail, she pushes him forward. The wolf takes a few steps, limping painfully. She pushes with her shoulder to steady him and he raises his tail and moves along the track she made. She runs ahead, barking, and returns to his side again. They stop to rest and she howls loudly. The notes rise and fall again and again. She hears the answer from the den, and alternately dances before her mate to encourage him, and behind him to give her support.

The young wolves rush forward, wagging their tails and touching noses with their parents. The mother scarcely glances at the food her yearlings brought in their throats and placed by the door. She can hear the cries of her hungry pups, and crawls out of sight into the tunnel.

The hungry, squirming, crying babies do not notice her cold wet coat, but nuzzle close to nurse. The whimpering changes to sucking noises and presently all is quiet in the nursery.

At last the mother wolf is free to crawl quietly out of the den to eat. She doesn't look at her mate who rests by the entrance or at the two young wolves that have taken up guard duty on top of the ridge. She eats until all the food is gone and then she approaches her mate and bites at his thick ruff. Their noses touch and he stands with difficulty and limpingly follows her inside out of the cold wind.

The fast-growing pups roll and tumble about in the underground nursery. They run along the tunnels and poke their noses into every corner. Their eyes are keen, their noses twitch with every new odor, and their ears turn about to receive every new sound. Finally, one small wolf puppy ventures along the tunnel and looks out—and just as quickly backs into the familiar passage. Soon several bright-eyed pups poke their heads out and look around.

The mother wolf asleep in the entrance in the bright sun raises

Wolf pup

her head and gives a low yip and all the pups tumble out and over their mother, the only familiar smell near. They run along the path a little way but return quickly when she barks. A raven's cry from a tree in the ravine sends them back into the den. Then each head appears and they rush out to explore again.

The female stands up so quickly that the startled pups run for the safety of the den. She barks softly and they return with their tails wagging. Together they stand waiting; the small bodies tremble and wriggle with excitement. Then, from far away they hear the clear notes increasing in tone and dropping quickly, and know it is the call of the hunters returning home. When their mother points her long, thin muzzle into the air to answer the

29

call, six small noses point skyward and they add their thin, high voices to the throaty song of the mother.

After being warmly greeted by the female and the pups, the hunters go to the side of the entrance and disgorge the food they have carried home in their throats. The female eats hungrily and the pups fight over bits of meat and bone. Weaning has begun.

Since wolves have no hands with which to carry anything, they must use their throats and jaws. The strong jaws can easily carry home a leg or thigh of a moose, but when the hunting has resulted in the capture of small animals such as mice, rabbits, and ground squirrels, they are swallowed and carried home to the hungry pups in the throat.

Because the wolf has a special stomach he must have meat or die, and he must hunt for and kill animals himself or he will starve. Wolves are large creatures and need lots of meat to satisfy their hunger. They are designed to chase and kill large animals. Learning all the skills of hunting is an important part of the training of the pups and a full-time job for both parents.

The mother wolf rests, stretched out at the den entrance, watching the busy inquisitive cubs explore every plant, every new odor, every strange sound. When they wander too far away she barks and they rush to her side and for a while climb over her, biting her mane and tail. She takes it good-naturedly. When they become bored they race to the top of the ridge where their father watches and naps. They play much rougher games with him, but when he's had enough he nips each pup that comes too near and, squealing, they run off to play with the two wolves nearer their age—that is, if the yearlings are nearby. Much of their time is spent practicing hunting not too far away.

As the afternoon passes, the mother becomes nervous and paces back and forth. The pups nap after their active play. The male wolf stretches and yawns and joins his mate at the den. He

30

When she barks, the pups return to her side

carries his tail high, she holds her head low, and they rub shoulders and touch noses. The pups join in the ceremony. With their shoulders touching, fur to fur, they start their evening concert. It is a happy social occasion and they seem to love every note of it. Not to be left out, the yearlings, off on a hunt of their own, come panting and bright-eyed to join in the songfest. For several minutes the sound is broadcast on the clear cold air and every creature for miles can hear it.

Abruptly they are silent and the dark gray male, tail held high, trots off down the slope, followed by the female close on his heels. The pups, barking excitedly, follow for about fifty feet, but turn and run toward their nursery with their tails between their legs when their mother gives a sharp bark. The light gray young

31

male follows the hunters with his tail waving jauntily, while the slender female yearling follows the six pups up the steep slope to the den. She stretches out in front of the entrance, for tonight she guards the young pups alone.

The time has come when the female can no longer feed the pups without eating more food than her mate and yearlings can bring home to her. Her stomach is often empty and her hair hangs down on her gaunt body. Besides, the pups need fresh meat, for their teeth are now strong and sharp.

The young female answers the call of the hunters now far away. The tired pups are soon asleep, but their "baby sitter" takes only cat naps as she has been taught to do.

Although the hunters travel fast, they pause now and then to sniff a tree or bush and to leave their own scent, dog fashion, for wolves are very conscious of their territory boundary lines and keep them well marked. Their range is about nine miles square—not very large for a family of wolves, but satisfactory when food is available.

Caribou watch for the hunting wolf

The three wolves trot along at about five miles an hour. It is good to stretch their legs. They could continue to travel all night, for they love to run. Often wolves pass many a deer or moose before attempting to make a kill, seemingly because they love to travel fast.

Because the hunters are very hungry they take every short cut they know and do not stop to rest. Since it is early spring they travel along the shores of the rivers and lakes and take well-marked trails that they have traveled often before. In winter they follow frozen rivers and use trails across open ridges and over hard-packed snowdrifts.

Their first encounter is with a moose, who whirls about to face them, and they quickly retreat because they know they are no match for a kicking moose. Their only chance to kill a moose is to make it run.

But luck is with the wolves this night and they startle a small herd of deer. One old deer becomes confused and does not move quickly enough. The large wolf springs at its neck and the other two wolves bring the deer down quickly. They could not have accomplished this had the deer been young and healthy. Deer can run faster than wolves and they know better than to try to outrun one.

The wolves set to their meal hungrily and only when they are satisfied do they begin to chew off large chunks of meat to cache for future use. The male carries a leg in his strong jaws for about half a mile along the river where he digs a shallow hole, places the meat in it, and covers it up for a future meal. The yearling takes a large piece to cache by the lake. Now there is food to satisfy the pups' growing appetite. All three swallow chunks of meat to carry back to the den for the rest of the family.

There is still much left on the carcass, but they trot off in the direction of the den. A fox slips quietly from the dark woods and

The wolf eats all he needs and then carries food home to his mate

begins to eat. Before the night ends, many creatures share the wolf kill, and by daylight the ravens clean it up. Nothing is wasted.

When the wolves reach the ravine below the den they stop long enough to notify those at home that they are safe and have food aplenty. Before they reach the top of the ridge they can hear the excited pups barking, and when they have finished the ceremonial greetings, the pups begin to stroke the necks of the hunters, their tails wagging. In response, the returning wolves lower their heads and disgorge the chunks of meat they carry. The pups eat noisily, fighting over the pieces of fresh meat. The male climbs slowly to the ridge to guard and cat nap. The other tired hunters are soon asleep.

The male wolf raises his head and looks about. He gets to his feet, tail held high. He seems to sense an intruder in his territory before he actually sees the large grizzly bear followed by her two cubs. He watches as they approach along the trail, investigating every dead tree stump. When the bears fail to turn off the path, the wolf barks sharply. The pups playing at the entrance of the den disappear inside. His mate follows, but watches from the opening.

The wolf descends quickly to the den and is met by the yearlings. After a slight pause he rushes down the trail, followed by the two young wolves. But the bear has no desire to meet the jaws of the wolf defending his family, and she and her cubs run for cover in a thicket nearby.

The wolves return to the den and howl several times as if to warn the bear to keep her distance hereafter. For a long time they can hear the grizzly family crashing through the undergrowth on the way to the ravine below. The wolves no doubt know how fierce a mother bear is when defending her young.

Had the danger been a man with a gun, the wolf would have run away from the den and howled to attract the attention of the hunter away from the den nursery. Wolves have been known to run for miles, occasionally showing themselves and howling, before they felt it was safe to circle around to the den again.

Perhaps it was the alarm of the bears, or the den may have become unclean or too small, or it may be that the time was right

Then the raven comes to pick the bones

for the move. At any rate, by late afternoon the mother becomes restless. She takes a pup in her large jaws, head to one side, tail on the other, and trots down the ridge past the nearest extra den and along the trail until she reaches a burrow near the ravine. She disappears inside and is soon out again, alone, and heads in the direction of the old den. The pups are barking excitedly, their tails wagging hard, when she reaches home. She scarcely pauses, but takes the nearest pup by the nape of the neck and heads down the ridge. She can hear the cries of the frightened pup she left in the strange den long before she reaches it.

It is twilight by the time the move had been made, and this night the hunter wolves go no farther than the nearest caches to obtain food for the family. Afterwards, the wolves touch noses and paw each other's ruffs and then sit with their shoulders touching and sing.

By daylight the pups spend hours exploring new smells and sounds, and new tastes too. They follow their parents along the trails, keeping close together, for everything is so strange. Their tails wag and they bark excitedly with each new experience. When they reach the ravine, the mother walks to the edge of the rippling water and, putting her head down, drinks long and loudly. The slurping noises and the strangeness send four pups racing back to the side of the male wolf. The two adventuresome ones rush forward and only a bark from the mother stops them at the very edge of the stream. They lap noisily as they take their first drink of fresh water. Now that the pups are about weaned, they must have water every day and there are many streams and lakes in their territory.

The pups run from side to side along the trail, barking at every sound and movement. They watch their father pounce quickly and turn with a field mouse in his jaws. The pups rush forward to

36

see it. They too listen and pounce, but catch nothing. Their lessons have started, but it is not easy to be a hunter, as they soon discover when dusk comes and they are tired and ready for sleep.

The wolf pups wake and begin to nuzzle their mother. They lick her face and bite her tail, then run along the tunnel to the entrance. Soon all the wolves are assembled and, with bodies touching and noses pointed upward, they break into their morning song. Ten voices make a good chorus and everyone appears to sing with real joy of living.

The songfest ends abruptly and the male leads the way along the trail toward the stream. The six wolf pups follow close to their mother and the two nearly grown wolves trot energetically

She steps into the stream and drinks noisily

along with their tails wagging. When they reach the water's edge they drink. Their noisy slurping is the only sound heard in the still early morning.

Although the pups do not know it, a new life has started for them. They will not return to their den again. Except for the denning time, wolves roam over their territory and sleep where and when tiredness overtakes them.

The wolf family moves slowly at an easy pace, for the pups sniff every plant and bark at every noise. The half-grown wolves go off on their own hunts and often return with some fresh meat for the pups, who rush to meet them, putting their paws on their necks and licking their faces. Then the pups fight over the meat and the bones which they love to chew—as all dogs do.

The yearlings take care of the wolf pups when the parents, no longer thin and ragged, go farther afield in search of food for all. The wolves often stay days in one rest spot near the kill when it is a big one. They sleep when they are full and eat again when they are hungry. Their travel periods become longer as the pups grow big and strong.

The wolf pups have by now grown coarse hair coats that range in color from black to buff. Their markings are distinctive and so are their personalities. Two are bolder than the others and often follow side trails for a long distance, sniffing and tasting everything until called back by a sharp bark. One pup is shy of everything strange. While all are energetic, three appear to be more playful and are always the last to stop for a rest. Two are smaller than the others and one pup seems to sulk. When he is bested in a game, he goes off alone and lies down with his head on his outstretched paws.

Yet all the wolf pups are affectionate and sociable. They rush to the top of a knoll to watch for the returning hunters and greet them with all the ceremony of licking faces, pawing shoulders,

The yearlings visit old caches looking for food

and rolling on the ground. Their tails wag hard and when they join in the greeting singsong, their howls are loud and strong.

Along the trails they meet other wolves. Sometimes it is a lone wolf whose mate has been killed and they chase it for half a mile. They know there is nothing to fear from such an animal, but they have an urge to chase any moving object and enough energy to do it.

The wolves leave the loafing place at dawn. A flock of ravens flies overhead and when the wolves stop to rest at about eleven o'clock the ravens settle on the ground nearby. The parents rest, stretched out but always alert. The pups, still full of energy, chase about in circles yelping and nipping each other. Then they drop to the ground to rest. The ravens fly up into the air and settle very near the pups, and the wolf pups bark and chase them away. The ravens return again and again to be chased, almost like a playful game.

About four o'clock the male rises, stretches, yawns, and touches noses with his mate. She paws his mane. The other wolves gather around to touch and be touched. The leader points his head upward and, starting with a low note, continues up the scale. The others join in and the whole effect is one of joy and well-being. The last low notes fade out and at once the wolves begin to travel single file behind the strong leader wolf. Thus begins their night's hunt.

Their first encounter is with a herd of deer who smell the wolves and run swiftly away. The pups rush ahead in pursuit, heedless of the low throaty warning of their parents. When they are exhausted the young wolves return with their tails between their legs. They have learned that a healthy herd is not worth the chase.

There are moose in the territory and sometimes a calf can be separated from its mother, but not without a real struggle. The first moose and calf the wolves see are too far away to chase, but the pups rush ahead and have to be called back with a sharp bark.

A yearling moose is another thing, and when one is sighted the whole wolf pack gives chase. But the young moose, not much larger than it was in the spring, has learned to protect itself and is now agile, alert, and fast. The adult wolves could outmaneuver the moose, but the pups are not yet strong enough for this chase. From this pursuit the pups at least learn what speed to expect from a young moose.

After a rest, the wolf hunters travel along the trail toward the lake, where the lead wolf stops suddenly. The others catch up quickly but silently. Near the edge of the lake a moose and her calf browse. They have not caught the smell of the wolves, and the large male wolf rushes forward to separate the two. The moose turn toward the lake where there is a chance of swimming to safety, but the wolves are between them and the water. The

The moose has not caught the smell of the wolf

mother pushes her calf back of her and faces the wolves, kicking in all directions. The pups are excited and rush in close—one so close that he is picked up by the great splayed hoof and thrown several feet. After a moment the stunned pup stands up and, with his tail between his legs, moves as far as possible from the thrashing creature. The wolves, still barking, back away from the moose. They know when they can't win. But the pup has learned the power in a moose's kick.

The wolves continue to the far side of the lake. The night is nearly over and they are tired and very hungry. Wolves can go a long time without food and often travel many, many miles without making a kill. However, their next encounter is with an old moose with well-worn teeth, who is not up to the energy and

41

The fawn hides safely in the thicket

hunger of the wolf family. The wolves make a quick kill and for the next few hours all of the family eat ravenously, tugging at the large carcass.

With their stomachs full they sleep nearby. Each wolf feeds twice during the first half day. One or two wolves are always eating while the others sprawl out in the sun. Ravens try to light every time the wolves leave the kill, but rise as soon as the next wolf moves toward the carcass. The wolves stay by the kill several days and when they finally leave there is little left on the bones. But a fox waits his turn and after he slinks away into the forest the ravens soon finish the job. The wolves travel only a short distance and return the next day to gnaw on the bones.

When the wolves rest it is usual for each one to hunt out the highest place around—a protruding rock, a stump, or a knoll, any point from which they can get a better view of the countryside. They may be looking for intruders or possible food, or it could be just out of curiosity. At any rate, one observing wolf sees a strange timber wolf and gives the alarm. The stranger is black, very tall, and trots along with his tail waving jauntily. He pauses to sniff a shrub and leave a scent, and continues along the trail as though boundary markings had no meaning.

The large male rushes forward with his strong jaws snapping; the other wolves stand ready to assist. The male needs no help and so they watch the creatures circle about each other. The younger wolf backs off the trail and stumbles. The older and stronger male stands over him. There is little doubt he could tear the intruder to pieces, but the wolf is not bloodthirsty. The fight ends suddenly, with the two standing and pressing shoulder to shoulder and growling. For a second their heads are close together, then the younger lowers his head and offers his neck to the teeth of the stranger, or so it seems.

One interpretation of this action is that the victor is bound by a wolf "code of honor" not to take advantage of the weaker animal. However, had the intruder been a threat to his family, no code would protect him. Besides, how can a wolf know where the jugular vein is located? Could it not be that lowering the head is merely taking a submissive position and that in itself takes the fight out of the stronger? Any boy knows that when he says "uncle" or "I give up" a fight is over. There is no merit for the stronger in continuing to fight the weaker, and so it must be with the wolf.

The intruding wolf departs quickly, with his tail between his legs, and the strong male turns toward the knoll with his tail held high. As he passes, each member of his pack lowers his head and

The wolf always goes to the highest place to look about

Each member of the pack greets the leader and shows deference

shoulders and stretches his forefeet forward as he acknowledges
their leader. This form of social behavior is common to many
groups of animals. In the wolf social order each member has his
special place. The pups have learned the rules they must follow
in group living.

Although wolves travel in family groups for most of the year,
when winter comes two or more family groups join together in
hunting packs. Such an arrangement has its advantages, for the
single wolf and for the small family, since naturally several
wolves can hunt more successfully than a mated pair and one
pup. It even helps a family of ten individuals, for in it there are

The wolf pack pushes through the heavy snow

but two adult wolves with many mouths to feed and winters are hard. A mated pair with one pup join the family group and are easily accepted. Now there are four strong adults, two nearly grown wolves, and seven pups that face the winter storms together.

The dark gray wolf, easily the leader, pushes through the chest-deep snow, with his tail held high. His mate follows with her tail erect too, and, stretched out for nearly a mile, are the other wolves, their tails swinging slowly. The going is hard and the leader stops to rest; the others catch up and approach him in a submissive posture. When he is rested he stands, shakes the snow from his coat, and continues breaking the trail. The pack rests when he rests and travels when he travels.

They reach the frozen river where the going is easier but he is careful to stay on the snow-covered ice, for he knows that snow-free ice is often new and thin. Winter trails soon pack hard and are easily followed at a trot of five miles an hour. Sometimes the wolves travel thirty-five miles in one night of winter hunting.

When a moose is sighted the leader rushes forward to threaten the animal and to make the attack. The moose finds it hard to make a stand in the deep snow and begins to run. Several of the pack run along the side of the fleeing animal, barking loudly; others lie down to wait for the kill to be made. After a chase of a few hundred yards, the lead wolf turns and barks and the chasers stop to allow the strong wolf to make the kill. The female joins her mate and they begin to eat. The others then join in, for there is plenty for all. When the kill is small, the youngest and weakest sometimes go hungry. When food is available the wolves gorge and then go several days without a kill. They seem to prefer hunger to using their energy to hunt anything as small as a rabbit.

After several days without a kill, the pack breaks up into small groups to hunt on their own. The lead pair takes their pups with them, the yearlings hunt together, and the other pair with their pup go on their own way. Now, smaller creatures are hunted to satisfy their immediate hunger.

At dusk the leader goes out on the ice and howls. The notes are low-pitched and drawn out. In five minutes the pups crowd about to howl with him. From the distance comes an answer. The mated pair with their pup emerge from the woodland, extend their paws forward in greeting, and join the others in their

47

The leader steps out on the ice and howls and the pack returns

calls Last come the yearlings, trotting along with their tails wagging and making throaty whimpers and yelps as if they didn't want to miss all the fun. Then, shoulder to shoulder, the wolves sing together in the gathering darkness.

The full significance of howling is not known. Wolves howl at the den on rising and leaving, and when they are hunting. They howl and respond when they are separated. Whether it is emotion or release of tension or to keep the pack together during a chase or to call the hunters together afterwards, the wolves seem always to love doing it. It is more like song than anything else, and instead of striking fear into the hearts of people it should cause them to raise their voices in answer, for it is one of the pure sounds of the wilderness—thrilling to some who hear it.

The winter is hard on the wolf family and there are always accidents—natural ones. Those of the young who survive are stronger and wiser and ready to take their responsibility in the family group. These wolves have not yet encountered the snow-mobile or poisoning programs that threaten their very existence. Perhaps they can live to add their beauty to our shrinking wilderness.

The coyote

The Coyote

The coyote stops on the crest of the hill and is silhouetted against the evening sky. He looks like a medium-sized collie dog, with the same long hair, tall slender legs, and bushy tail. However, this is no dog, although they are related, but a small wolf about a third the size of the gray timber wolf. He is a coyote—and you can pronounce it with either two or three syllables. Because he prefers open country, the early settlers in America called him "prairie wolf" to distinguish him from his larger relative, who stays as much as possible in wooded places.

A second coyote climbs the hill slowly, stopping often to sniff a bush to see who has passed along this way recently. Like all her kin, she adds her "calling card" from a scent gland situated at the base of her tail. Her light buff-gray coat with its rust shades makes her blend with her surroundings. Her long tail wags with pleasure as she approaches her mate. For a little while they stand close together, with the changing sunset colors behind them. They are graceful and slender and stand two feet tall at the shoulders and measure four feet from their long pointed faces to their black-tipped tails.

Then, for no apparent reason, they point their narrow muzzles into the air and make a mournful sound, starting with a long high-pitched note and ending with a series of yips. Across the valley comes an answering call, and another from farther away. For a few minutes the sounds echo from all the hills around.

The coyotes give a mournful sound

When the last yelp dies away, the male trots off down toward the ravine with his mate following close behind.

Their den—one they had used the spring before—was once the home of a badger, who was such an excellent digger that the coyote has few changes to make to turn it into a perfect nursery for her pups. She digs an additional entrance that is hidden by a bush and pushes the dirt along the twenty-foot tunnel to make a mound at the old entrance. She scratches a small ventilating hole directly above the nursery chamber halfway along the tunnel. She carries in her mouth a few bits of dry grass in a half-hearted attempt to make the nursery more comfortable, but it is hardly enough to do any good. For the past few weeks she has cleaned out several dens to use if she needs them, but it is in this old badger hole that her five pups are born on a chilly April day.

They are soft balls of brownish-gray fur with their eyes tightly closed and their round ears flat to their heads. The pads on their tiny feet are light pink. For the first couple of days she stays with them all the time, except when she goes to the entrance to eat a squirrel or mouse brought by her mate. The male, with his tail wagging happily, watches her eat. At a whimper from the den, the female returns to her pups.

The cry comes from one small creature that has managed to squirm out of contact with the others. When the coyote pups are touching they are silent, but when she approaches they squirm about and whine until she settles down to nurse them.

After a few days of eating only the rodents her mate brings her, the female coyote joins him in his hunt in the early morning and late evening. When she returns, she examines the ground around the entrance before entering to feed her family. She does

The female examines the ground before entering the den

53

not remain with the pups all the time now, but stays with he mate in a hidden spot near the den where they both can be o guard duty. They watch one direction with their eyes, whil their ears turn in another direction to catch every sound and thei keen noses are aware of every new smell. If the wind changes they shift their watching places. When it is time to return to he pups, the female stretches and yawns and makes a wide circl against the wind in the direction of the den. When she reache the entrance, she steps around the mound of dirt and disappear inside the burrow toward her whimpering hungry pups.

The young coyotes grow rapidly. At ten days their milk teetl appear and the pads of their feet turn black; after two week their eyes are open. They are curious about everything and se they follow their mother along the tunnel to play around th door. They are weak and wobbly, like all dog puppies, and the

The den was once the home of a badger

The young coyote pups grow rapidly

either run eagerly toward every sound with their tails wagging happily or they back away, frightened, with their tails between their legs.

Soon they are pouncing on insects, trying to catch them. When their mother returns from a hunt they run to meet her and paw at her throat and mouth. She gives a big heave and deposits half-digested food on the ground before the pups. They eat hungrily, for their weaning has started. Later, they follow her into the nursery to finish off the meal with milk, and then they sleep.

By the time the coyote pups are five weeks old they run along the well-marked trail they know their parents will take when they return from their early morning hunting trip. They pounce

*The mother rabbit covers her
nest when she leaves*

on grasshoppers and stalk field mice as they wait and keep watch
on a small knoll. The parents carry rodents in their teeth and
these the pups fight over. Then the hunters regurgitate swallowed food, their means of bringing meat back to their hungry
young. The parents watch while the pups eat and then the
mother rolls over and lets them nurse briefly. When she stands
up and moves away, they follow, trying to continue the meal.
She growls and they shrink backward and follow her to the den.

At nearly dusk the adult coyotes stand up and stretch and become tense, their ears high and their pointed noses quivering. A
long way off a man comes across the field in their direction. The
female looks at her pups sniffing at rodent tunnels, and barks.
The pups flatten out on the ground with their small faces on their
paws. They do not move a muscle. They wait and the parents
watch. There is a loud bang, but the pups do not panic. After a
long time the parents move quietly and the pups start to meet
them. A low growl stops them and they flatten out again.

The male lowers his head and takes one pup by the scruff of

The pups learn to catch insects

the neck and moves in the direction of a new den. The female carries the second pup, and before the coyotes depart for their evening hunt, the five pups are safely installed in a new home.

The pups have hunting lessons every day in the meadow and both parents are excellent teachers. Each pup learns to move slowly toward a sound, then to freeze for a moment before pouncing. At first he often misses, but tries again. When he learns to catch a mouse, he must also learn to hold it securely against the ground until it is possible to get it into his mouth. It is not easy and often the frightened rodent gets safely away.

Rabbits, although harder to catch, make such a good meal that

The wood rat hurries out of its burrow to find food

*The coyote pups learn that they can attack deer if they are clever enough
to separate the mother from her young*

they are worth the trouble, and when the coyote pups learn to
hunt in pairs, even they are easily caught. The pups are smart
and they soon learn that rabbits tend to run in a circle. By cutting
across the circle they can catch up with and head off the rabbit.
Then, they learn that they can attack even a deer and her young,
if one of the pair attracts the attention of the mother while the
other attacks the young. Slowly the coyote pups begin to use
their brains rather than just their brawn. They watch attentively
as their father walks among grazing cattle, easily catching any
frightened rodent or rabbit flushed out.

There are many small creatures in the hunting territory. Had
there not been, the coyotes would have moved on, for they fol-

low a food supply. The pups learn to eat berries and thorn apples, persimmons and chokecherries, and of course they know when watermelons are ripe. It isn't that coyotes like everything they eat, it is that they learn to eat everything edible. It is this ability to adapt to whatever food is available that has made it possible for the coyote to spread far and wide.

If food is available the coyote does not move far from its birthplace, and such is the case with this family. By autumn the pups are as large as their parents and wear the same richly colored coats. Their undercoat is tan and two inches thick; their overcoat is made of guard hairs three and a half inches long, tipped with brown or black. Now it is time for the family group to separate.

The mated pair stays together; the pups are often seen hunting together in the same neighborhood where they were born. It is here they learned where to find food and where the best hiding places are. The coyote young know they need not fear the antelope and deer and badger. They understand that the ravens,

The mother squirrel watches her baby very closely

Even the whitefoot mouse is hunted when coyotes are really hungry

always ready to share their food, also fly up and give warning if there is danger near. They know better than to trust the eagle, they keep clear of the cougar and bear, and they know about the man with a gun.

The young coyotes have mock fights in the snow, much as they did when they were a month old, but now they look more serious. The fight ends when one animal is forced down on his back and side. Coyotes do not need a well-defined social order when they hunt together so successfully and food is plentiful. The submissive play-fighting is much the same as that of dogs or boys.

A pair of coyotes discovers a limping deer shot by a hunter. The creature is too weak to run in the deep snow. The kill is quick and easy and the coyotes eat hungrily. One coyote lifts his head and howls, and there is an answer and then another. Soon, two coyotes appear from opposite sides of the clearing and join in the feast.

Could the call have been an invitation to dinner? There is no way of knowing, but before long, seven coyotes are eating together. Could this be the coyote family gathered to share a kill? When all are filled and there is still meat left, one of the coyotes digs into the snow and buries a piece. Five of the coyotes trot off in different directions toward the woods, leaving one pair that gives two long howls that float off in the clear cold air. There are several answers. Were they responses, or echoes from the hills?

Coyotes have trouble in deep snow because of their short legs —and so have difficulty catching rabbits if the snowfall is heavy. When the snow crusts over, they can walk on top and attack even a large deer that breaks through and flounders about. When the cold season is long and hard and food scarce, the litters are small.

All winter the coyote serenades continue, and everywhere men grab their guns and go hunting the small wolf of the prairies. There is no record that a coyote has ever attacked a man, yet he is considered a number one villain. He will kill a sheep or a goat when they are available; meat is meat and he knows no better.

In the snow, the snowshoe rabbit can outrun a coyote

The coyote is silhouetted against the sky

He preys on the weak of the herd, the starving, or the wounded. Rodents and rabbits are his main food supply, and where the coyote lives these creatures that feed upon farmers' crops are kept in control. Well-informed farmers would rather lose a sheep now and then than have rats eat their grain. Yet they still seem intent on wiping out the coyote.

Once there was a bounty for coyotes, and man killed them for money. Now, there are few bounties left and no need for them, since the man with a gun shoots at every coyote he sees or hears just for the fun of it. A *New York Times* editorial reports that "ranchers in Florida drove coyote pups into a burrow, fished them out with long wires, and then held them in an iron cage for twenty-four hours without water in ninety-degree heat in the vain hope that the coyote parents would return to rescue them and be trapped themselves."

The coyote can and does outsmart man and his guns, but can he cope with such barbaric actions, or the poisoning programs, or airplanes that shoot him down when he hunts, or snowmobiles that can follow his well-beaten tracks to his den? The world is more beautiful "where coyotes howl and the wind blows free."

The Red Fox

The more the fox is hunted, the smarter it becomes—or so it seems. He has been able to expand his range until it stretches over mountains, plains, and deserts.

You may see the sharp-witted and beautiful fox trotting across a field and disappearing into a nearby woodland. This sly creature has no wish to meet the man with a gun, and so he tries not to be seen. Like his relatives, the coyote and wolf, the fox will not harm you even if you meet it on a woodland path. He will look at you a moment with his ears erect, then drop his head and trot off to the nearest cover.

If you should discover a fox in your neighborhood, then you can hold your head a little higher, for you are experiencing something very precious—the beauty of the wilderness. It is a great temptation to share the thrill of discovery, but learn to be careful to whom you tell your secret. Remember that there are plenty of people whose first thought will be: "A wild creature! Where's my gun?"

To learn about the beautiful fox, let's go to the woods of North America where the red fox has been studied in the wilderness that has always been its home.

It is midwinter and very cold, but the fox is clothed to endure

The red fox

extremely low temperatures. Beneath his long winter coat is a thick wooly undercoat made especially to trap air, and so it serves to keep the creature warm. His feet are kept warm by his winter "shoes" of heavy fur that almost hide his toe pads. Because of the cold, his rust-colored fur stands out from his body, making him look larger than he really is. Actually, a man's fingers on one hand can encircle his body, were it not for the thick coat he wears. The color of the fox's coat can range from yellow to red or silver or black; the creature wearing it is much the same in its habits. The red fox, however, always looks as if it were wearing long black stockings on his legs.

The fox looks all about him. He licks his sharp black nose, the better to "read" the wind currents; his pointed ears stand erect. Satisfied that all is well, he curls up in the snow close to a rock and puts his magnificent fur tail over his body and face. Tired after a night of hunting and snug under his tail blanket, he drops

The arctic fox in its protective white coat is much like other foxes

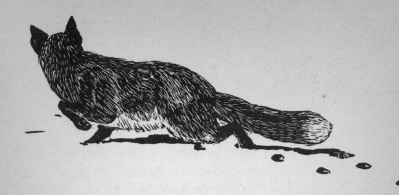

You may see a fox disappear into the woods

The fox curls up for a sleep

The fox jumps on stiff legs and catches a mouse

into a deep sleep and his breathing becomes slower and very regular.

Curled up into a ball of fur, the red fox looks even smaller than he is. A fully grown fox weighs from ten to fifteen pounds and stands about sixteen inches high. The body plus the long bushy tail measures about a yard.

When we see the red fox again he is accompanied by a companion—his mate. The smaller fox steps into his tracks and they zigzag through the snow with their ears alert and their heads bent, listening for the slightest sound. They stop often to sniff a

A rabbit rushes for shelter

branch sticking out of the snow, and to leave a bit of scent of their own before continuing on their way.

The female fox jumps forward on stiff legs and raises her head with a long-tailed shrew in her jaws. It isn't much, but she is hungry and eats it. She sniffs the ground and begins to dig into an old cache where she finds a long-buried muskrat and fills her stomach. What is left she puts back into the hole and pulls the snow over it with her nose. Then she leaves a scent and moves on.

The skunk has a meal

The gray fox watches a mouse hole, ready to pounce

A passing skunk sniffs out the buried food and has a free meal, but the skunk does not store food and so what is left when he is finished is soon found by a flock of crows and a hawk, all calling loudly as they dine on the fox's leftovers. There is no waste in nature.

The male chases a rabbit who hesitates a second at the entrance of a hole, giving the fox just the advantage needed and a good satisfying meal. Later, he tears with his paws at a stump where he can hear the squeaks of a deer mouse, and then gives up and leaves his scent. While he waits for his mate to join him he sniffs around a badger hole, makes a stiff-legged jump and catches a vole which he drops in front of his mate when she reaches him.

At daybreak the two foxes curl up close together with their tails spread over them to keep warm. Blowing snow half covers the two fur balls, but they sleep snugly.

In early March the fox pair goes house hunting. They investi-

The fox brings food to feed his mate

gate a number of abandoned burrows, sniffing about first to discover if they are occupied. Then they dig away the snow and leaves and disappear inside. They clean the hole out, leave their scent, and trot on to find another hole that could serve as a nursery den.

The fox looks for a suitable den

The parents watch over the pups when they are playing

Like their cousins, the wolf and the coyote, the foxes prepare several extra homes. One is used for a nursery for the fox pups and, like their relatives, the male provides the food for his mate while she feeds the young and keeps them warm. The five pups are a month old when they can be seen wrestling and pouncing on each other at the entrance to the den. Both parents hunt and bring back mice, squirrels, and rabbits. There is always a tug of war over the food and the winner runs into the den to eat the prize.

The foxes are always on guard. An eagle circling overhead sends the pups scampering to safety. A bobcat almost catches a

The pups sun at the entrance to the den

pup whose curiosity takes him too far from home. This fright causes the family to move to a new den. Now they have more freedom and the pups get more lessons in hunting and safety. They have much to learn if they are to become independent by fall.

In early June the pups play in the fields. They make elaborate stalks and pounce on imaginary mice. They stretch out in the sun and scratch. They walk across the stream on a log and return safely. They follow their parents on short hunting trips and practice catching insects while the mother hunts small birds in the bushes nearby. The world is full of sounds and smells to investigate. They sniff out a cache and dig up a shrew and bury it again. "School" is never out, and when the foxes are tired they stretch out in the sun and rest, and even take short cat naps, but they are always alert to danger.

Like the wolves and coyotes, the fox family eventually leaves the nursery den for good and hunts all night over a wide range. The foxes curl up to sleep at sunrise wherever they happen to be.

The fox stalks his prey

Soon the pups have learned to catch rabbits—their main food—as well as their parents, and they know all the holes in which to run for safety. Their wits are keen. The slow and the weak have no chance, and only quick, healthy, and bright fox pups get past their training days.

Some of the pups settle nearby, adding their beauty to the wilderness; others travel many miles to find an area that offers safety and enough food.

The baby rabbits nearby are very quiet

The fox, too, is a hunter who must have fresh meat. He may kill a pheasant that a so-called sportsman wants to kill with a gun. Yet studies prove that game birds flourish where the fox hunts, but disappear from fields and woods when the man with the gun hunts them.

The hunter fox is not large enough to kill a big animal, but can take a chicken from a farmer's coop. Today, wise farmers know that by killing insects and rodents that devour crops, the fox does a great service. In places where the fox has been destroyed, leaving the rodents unchecked, farmers lose millions of dollars in crops.

A news item best illustrates the shortsightedness of man and the possible fate of the fox. In the summer of 1968, a red fox shot in the woods of Maine was found to have rabies. There was a chance that town dogs, allowed to roam freely through the woods with a hunter out to kill anything that moves, might come across a fox with rabies. So a poisoning program was started. This is how it works. Squirrels and rabbits are killed and filled with poison and placed on trails known to be frequented by the fox.

The pups watch the mother and learn to pounce

The pups quickly learn to catch insects

The unsuspecting fox eats the food with its poison and travels some distance before it dies. Other small meat-eaters like the skunks and raccoons then eat the poisoned rabbit or squirrel left by the fox and also are poisoned. And all the meat-eaters, in a never-ending chain, eat the poisoned flesh of the dead fox and the skunk and raccoon, and die. The hawk and the crow spread the poison still farther, until countless creatures for miles around are dead, and the woods become silent—because man, the meddler, has been at work.

The fox, like its relatives the wolf and the coyote, has a place in the scheme of things. When you see one of these lovely creatures you have experienced a wonderful thing, for where the beautiful fox lives, a precious bit of wilderness exists.

Prints of the forefoot of a wolf, a coyote, and a fox

Timber wolf
Approximate Length: 5″

Coyote
Approximate Length: 2½″

Red fox
Approximate Length: 2¼″

Index